MW01045109

is a strange feeling that links us mysteriously to someone, though we
unable to explain why or how. It is made of a thousand subtle emo-
a thousand almost imperceptible details that combined, create a
ivity that is heightened by the mere presence of the that other, unique
n who transforms and lifts our reality into another realm. When you
confident that you can take on any challenge life may bring you

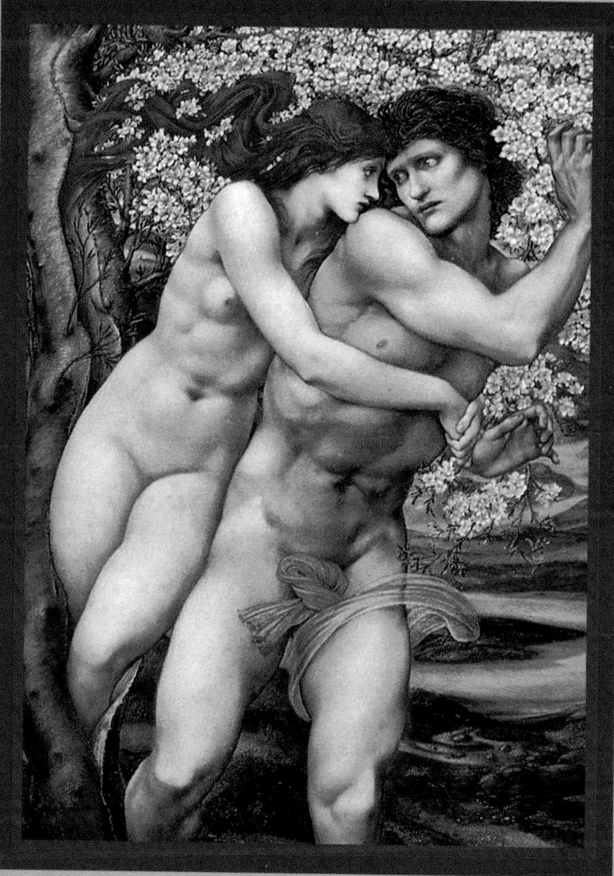

iends
milar-
ife is
se of
anges
vever,
f our
Each
pre-
deli-
vildly,
blind
oving
s any
Love
e are
ns, a
itivity
erson
feel
way,
itably

hat you are officially in love. And strangely but similarly, when you
rmented or melancholic, when you complain that life is dreary and
hose same friends will suspect that love is the cause of all your
ns. Love, though so exalting, more often than not plunges us into a
oxical state where joy and sadness alternate. However, even when
in an extreme state of doubt as to the sincerity of our "other one"

ove is a strange feeling that links us mysteriously to someone, thou
are unable to explain why or how. It is made of a thousand subtle
ions, a thousand almost imperceptible details that combined, create a
itivity that is heightened by the mere presence of the that other, u
erson who transforms and lifts our reality into another realm. The

feel
way,
inevit
when
drea
all ye
us in
even
"othe
of u
parei
cious
when
eye t
anoth
other
is a
unat
thous
that
who t
confi
when
think

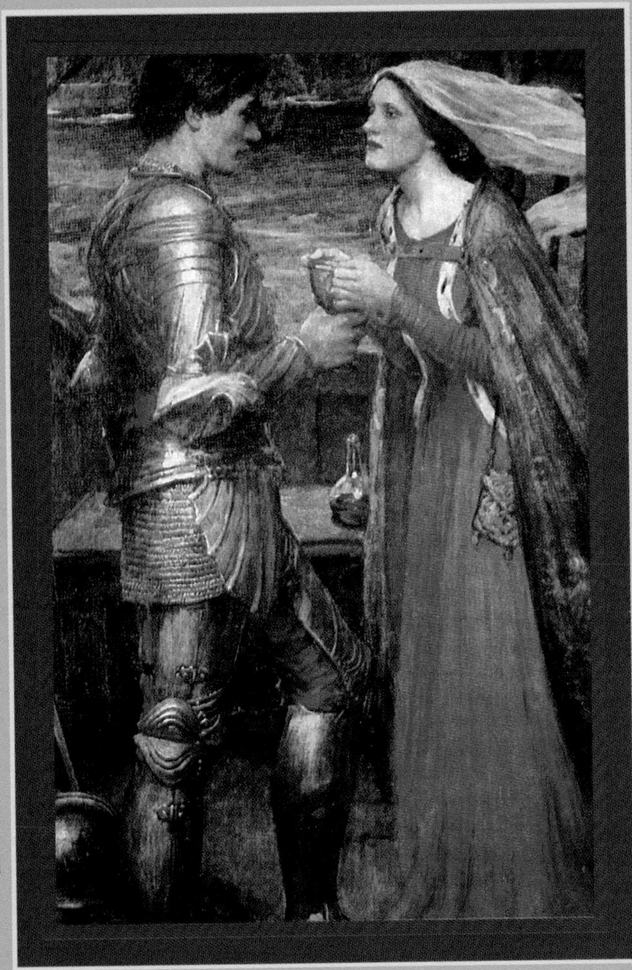

look tormented or melancholic, when you complain that life is drea
gray, those same friends will suspect that love is the cause of a
concerns. Love, though so exalting, more often than not plunges us
paradoxical state where joy and sadness alternate. However, eve
we are in an extreme state of doubt as to the sincerity of our "othe

TRUE
LOVE

This book belongs to

_____

© 2000 Modus Vivendi Publishing Inc.
All rights reserved.

Published by:
Modus Vivendi Publishing Inc.
3859 Laurentian Autoroute
Laval, Quebec
Canada H7L 3H7
or
2565 Broadway, Suite 161
New York, New York 10025

Translation: Brenda O'Brien
Cover: Marc Alain

Picture Credits: © 1997 Wood River Gallery and SuperStock

Legal Deposit: 3rd Quarter, 2000
National Library of Canada

Canadian Cataloguing in Publication Data
Therrien, Laurette
  True Love
  (Heartfelt Series)
  Translation of: Histoire d'amour.
  ISBN: 2-89523-027-7
  1. Love. 2. Love – Pictorial works. I. Title. II. Series
BF575.L8.T4613 2000   152.4'1   C00941189-5

Canadä We acknowledge the financial support of the Government
of Canada through the Book Publishing Industry Development
Program (BPIDP) for our publishing activities.

TRUE
LOVE

Laurette Therrien

MV Publishing

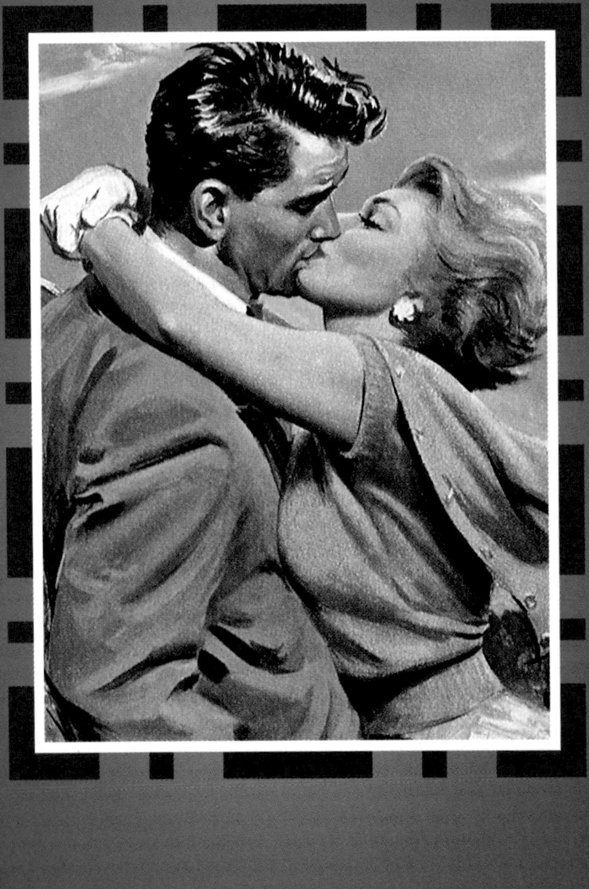

"Love looks not with the eyes, but with the mind;
And therefore is winged Cupid painted blind."

William Shakespeare,
A Midsummer Night's Dream

Love is a strange feeling that links us mysteriously to someone, though we are unable to explain why or how. It is made of a thousand subtle emotions, a thousand almost imperceptible details that, combined, create a sensitivity that is heightened by the mere presence of the other, unique person who transforms and lifts our reality into another realm. When you feel confident that you can take on any challenge life may bring your way, when you are sure that you can move mountains, your friends inevitably think that you are officially in love. And strangely but similarly, when you look tormented or melancholic, when you complain that life is dreary and gray, those same friends will suspect that love is the cause of all your concerns.

Love, though so exalting, more often than not plunges us into a paradoxical state where joy and sadness alternate. However, even when we are in an extreme state of doubt as to the sincerity of our "other one", love keeps us loyal, love keeps us from turning away. Each of us has sought that most heartfelt of all emotions. We are prepared to cope with the worst of torments to maintain it, to savour each delicious, delightful, delirious moment.

When our heart beats madly, wildly, when we tremble with the pleasure that love brings, we willingly turn a blind eye to worries and uncertainty. Nothing compares to the ecstasy of loving another human being. The feeling is incomparable and far outweighs any other experience we may live on our tiny planet and in our universe.

Jewels

The darling one was naked, and knowing my wish,
Had kept only the regalia of her jewelry
Whose resonant charms can lure and vanquish
Like a Moorish slave-girl's in her moment of glory.

A world of dazzling stones and of precious metals
Flinging, in its quick rhythm, glints of mockery
Ravishes me into ecstasy, I love to madness
The mingling of sounds and lights in one intricacy.

Naked, then, she was to all of my worship,
Smiling in triumph from the heights of her couch
At my desire advancing, as gentle and deep
As the sea sending its waves to the warm beach.

Her eyes fixed as a tiger's in the tamer's trance,
Absent, unthinking, she varies her poses
With an audacity and wild innocence
That gave a strange pang to each metamorphosis.

Her long legs, her hips, shining smooth as oil,
Her arms and her thighs, undulant as a swan,
Lured my serene, clairvoyant gaze to travel
To her belly and breasts, the grapes of my vine.

With a charm as powerful as an evil angel
To trouble and calm where my soul had retreated,
They advanced slowly to dislodge it from its crystal
Rock, where its loneliness meditated.

(...)

With the hips of Antiope, the torso of a boy,
So deeply was the one form sprung into the other
It seemed as if desire had fashioned a new toy.
Her farded, fawn-brown skin was perfection to
either!

And the lamp having at last resigned itself to death,
There was nothing now but firelight in the room,
And every time a flame uttered a gasp for breath
It flushed her amber skin with the blood of its bloom!

Charles Baudelaire

A Kiss

"A kiss, when all is said, what is it?
An oath that is ratified, a sealed promise,
A heart's avowal claiming confirmation,
A rose-dot on the 'i' of 'adoration,'
A secret that to mouth, not ear, is whispered,
Brush of a bee's wing, that makes time eternal,
Communion perfumed like the spring's
wild flowers,
The heart's relieving in the heart's outbreathing,
When to the lips the soul's flood rises, brimming!"

Edmond Rostand
Cyrano de Bergerac, Excerpt

"Love is not only an emotion,
It is also an art."

Balzac

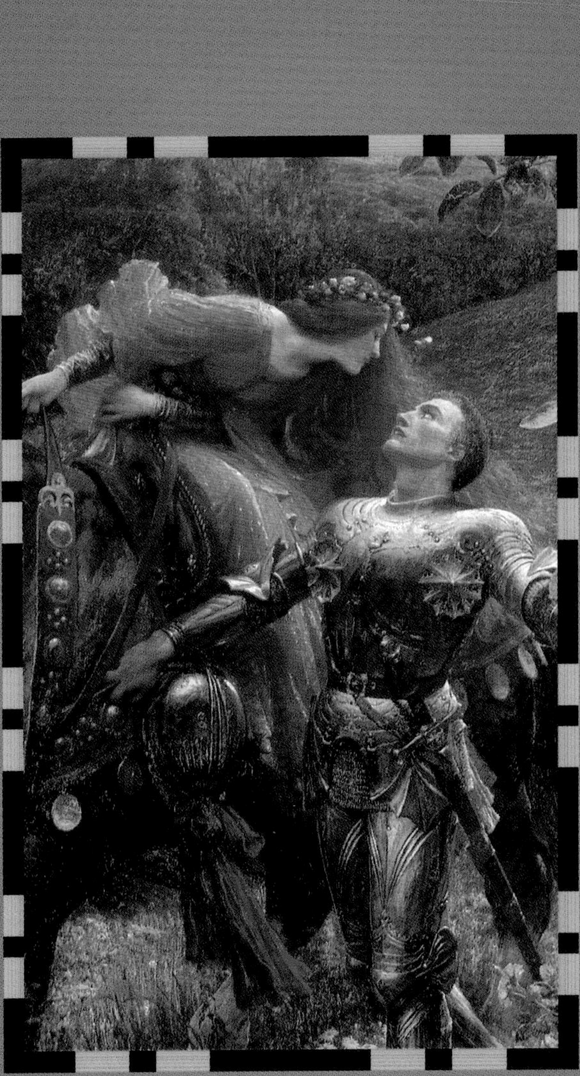

Ecstasy

"I fell into her arms, inebriated with love and happiness, and for seven hours I gave her the most positive of proof of my ardor and the emotion she inspired in me. She taught me nothing in matters of material truth; but oh! so much in her sighs, her transports of delight, her ecstasy, in feelings of a kind unable to develop but in a soul sensitive to the most tender of moments. I varied our pleasure in a thousand ways and I amazed her by showing her that she was susceptible to more pleasure than she ever could have imagined."

Casanova, *Memoirs*

Did you know that...

Casanova's name is known throughout the world and many people believe that the intriguing courtesan is a fictional character. On the contrary, he truly existed and he was the main driving force behind his own celebrity.

Giovanni Giacomo Casanova de Seingalt (1725-1798) was a French-speaking Italian. An adventurer, he travelled throughout Europe, practising several trades including writer of memoirs, soldier, diplomat, financier, publicist, secret agent, librarian.

Casanova was intent on collecting amorous conquests. As a matter of fact, he owes his fame to the description of his unbridled lovemaking sessions in an autobiography entitled *Memoirs or The Story of My Life*, an erotic and joyous confession tinged with a magnificent sense of freedom, published in its entirety for the first time in the early 1960s.

Did you know that...

Throughout history, the language of flowers has been very closely linked with love.

Abor Vitae - Unchanging friendship.
Camellia, White - Loveliness.
Candytuft - Indifference.
Carnation, Deep Red - Pity my poor heart.
Clover, 4-leaf - Be mine.
Columbine - Folly.
Columbine, Purple - Resolved to win.
Daisy - Innocence.
Fern - Fascination.
Forget-me-not - True love. Forget me not.
Fuchsia, Scarlet - Taste.
Geranium, Scarlet - Consolation.
Geranium, Rose - Preference.
Heliotrope - Devotion.
Ivy - Fidelity.
Lily-of-the-Valley - Return of happiness.
Mignonette - Your qualities surpass your charms.
Peach Blossoms - I am your captive.
Pear Blossoms - Affection.
Rose - Love.
Rose, Yellow - Jealousy.
Rose, White - I am worthy of you.
Tuberose - Dangerous pleasures.
Witch Hazel - A spell.

I strolled about and picked flowers,
For my home, for my loves.
They are joy and sunshine.
Their gentle beauty
Reminds me of your love.
Today, I am not alone.

L.T.

Love, True Love

Their resistance had reached its limits; they had set a secret rendezvous. Fuel added to a fire that had blazed since their first meeting, in a café where he worked as a waiter.

They were young, almost beautiful, and they could have been carefree had fate not catapulted them into a life that resembled them not. They had little in common and they were aware of their differences, but they had the firm resolve to quench a thirst that could find an outlet only in the freedom they at last embraced, touched and astonished, incredulous in the face of the brutality of their situation, so fraught with obstacles even as it brought them together.

They had made no promises in the past and the future held no promises. They had simply admitted to the urgent need to give in to wild desire. A desire that had to be fulfilled, no matter the loss, no matter the threat involved.

The room was tiny, dark and sparse, but they took no notice. They would have made love to one another anywhere, especially because this was the very first time, but especially because it was the very last time. So be it.

They were found the next night, intertwined in death's infinite clasp, enjoying the ultimate gift that only true lovers can share.

L.T.

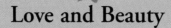

Love and Beauty

"Heaven has made me, so you say, beautiful,
and so much so that in spite of yourselves my
beauty leads you to love me; and for the love
you show me you say, and even urge, that I am
bound to love you. By that natural
understanding which God has given me I know
that everything beautiful attracts love, but I
cannot see how, by reason of being loved, that
which is loved for its beauty is bound to love
that which loves it; besides, it may happen that
the lover of that which is beautiful may be ugly,
and ugliness being detestable, it is very absurd
to say, "I love thee because thou art beautiful,
thou must love me though I be ugly." But
supposing the beauty equal on both sides, it
does not follow that the inclinations must be
therefore alike, for it is not every beauty that
excites love, some but pleasing the eye without
winning the affection; and if every sort of
beauty excited love and won the heart, the will
would wander vaguely to and fro unable to
make choice of any; for as there is an infinity of
beautiful objects there must be an infinity of
inclinations, and true love, I have heard it said,
is indivisible, and must be voluntary and
not compelled."

Cervantes, *Don Quixote*

"When a woman is faithful, she is admired;
but there are modest women who do not have
the vanity of wanting to be admired."

Marivaux

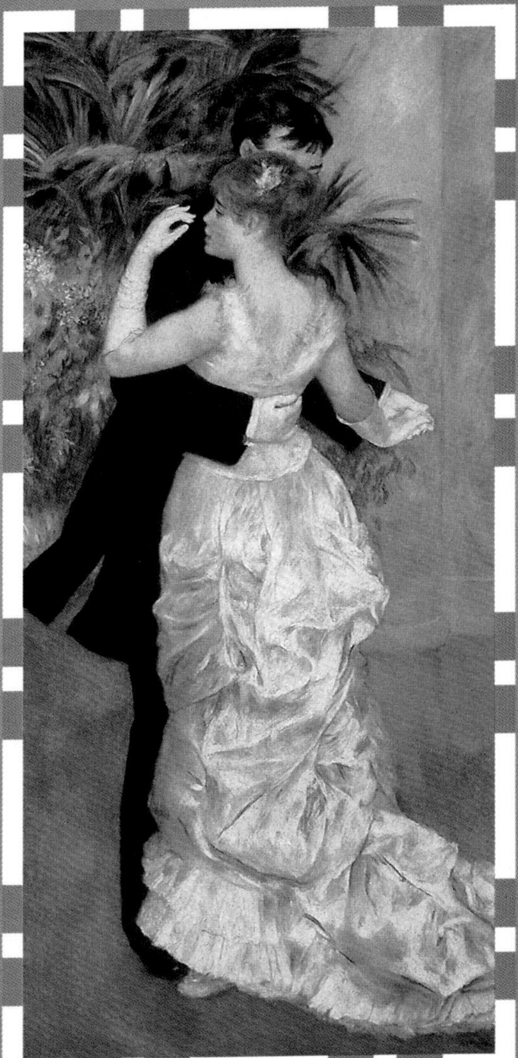

"How do I love thee? Let me count the ways.
I love thee to the depth and breadth and height
My soul can reach, when feeling out of sight
For the ends of Being and ideal Grace.
I love thee to the level of everyday's
Most quiet need, by sun and candlelight.
I love thee freely, as men strive for Right;
I love thee with the passion put to use
In my old griefs, and with my childhood's faith.
I love thee with a love I seemed to lose
With my lost saints, —
I love thee with the breath,
Smiles, tears, of all my life! — and, if God choose,
I shall but love thee better after death."

Elizabeth Barret Browning

"Within you I lose myself
Without you I find myself
Wanting to be lost again."

Unknown

"Love is not love that alters
when it alteration finds."

Shakespeare

"If I could reach up and hold a star for every
time you've made me smile, the entire evening
sky would be in the palm of my hand."

Unknown

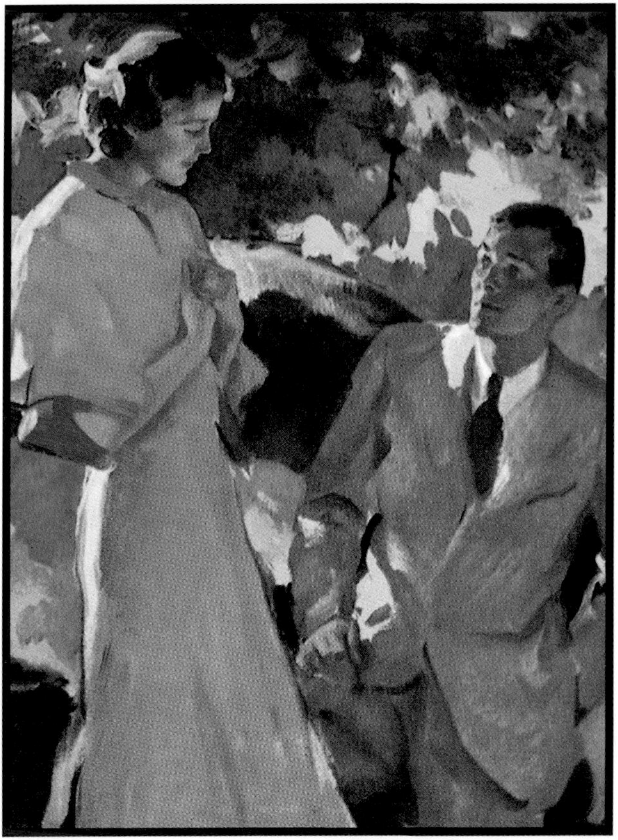

A Sweet Admission

You were everything:

    My feather dancing in the wind
    My wandering ways
    My quest for new heights
    My search for the depths of feeling
    My tiger's balm
    My autumn tour
    My tightrope
    My magical idea
    My sudden anger
    My most treasured of friends
    My thousand and one nights
    My botanical gardens
    My chinook wind
    My blizzard
    My tornado
    My turn of the century
    You were the white orchid worn
    by the heartbroken bride
    and my concrete-bound blossom.
    Strong. Well armed.
    And I, disarmed. Weak.

You were everything.

My blushing flesh
    My rich, lush fruit
    My unseeing eyes.
    A Titan, then a tyrant.
    That I had not foreseen.

You were everything.

                               L.T.

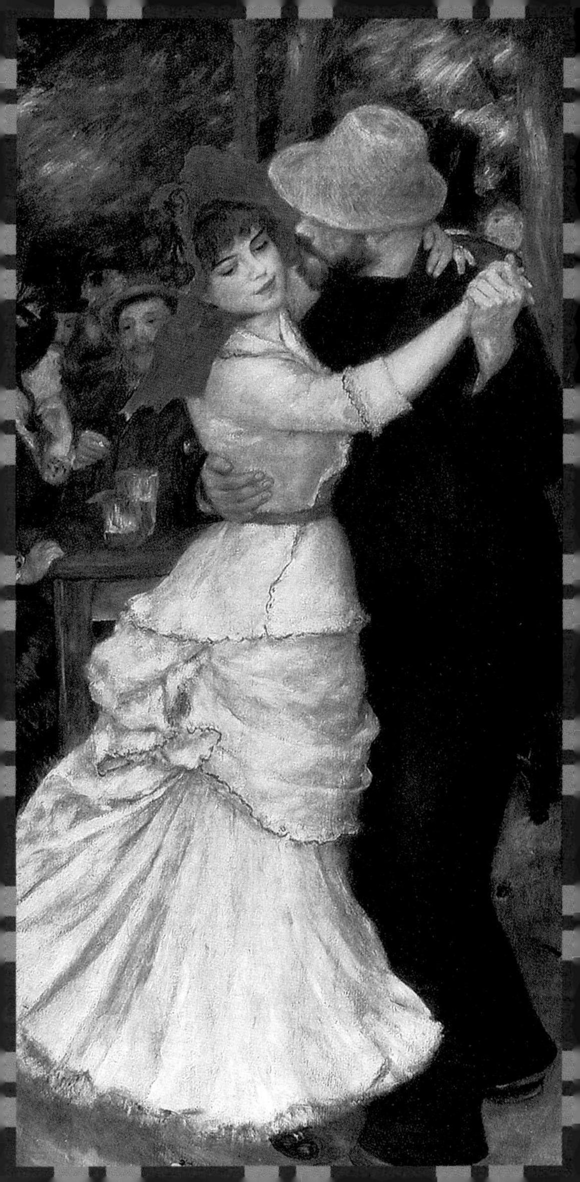

Works of the Flesh

You called him at work, he hadn't a minute to himself, overworked as usual, burdened with the many tasks at hand. He seemed distant, unavailable, he hesitated before telling you it was impossible, not now, before hanging up with the promise to drop by tomorrow.

But you knew the strength, the violence and the pull in your own words. Your voice, the sound of your breath over the telephone line, the urgency of your desire went directly to his heart, and he was no longer able to concentrate on the things he had to do.

Sure of yourself, confident, you stayed beside the phone, which soon rang with the most insistent of rings. He voice was not the same, altered as it was with a thundering desire. He would be there soon! Not a single minute to lose. It would be a celebration, it would be a feast!

Desires and Delights

A full-bodied and heady red wine or his favourite port.

A few cheeses, the richest, the creamiest:
- a melt-in-your-mouth brie;
- a gorgonzola on a tender lettuce leaf;
- a ripened goat's cheese on a bed of tender and young radicchio;

and since you meticulously planned everything the day before, a generous salad of calamari or hearts of palm in a vinaigrette flavoured with fennel.

Have no fear of excess.
In love, greed is the best of all possible avenues.

You, Me...

- What would you like? Pearls, a diamond?
- I don't have a price, said the woman, turning on her heels.
- But I'm crazy about you, answered the man, his back to the wall. I am totally serious...
- All you can talk about is giving me a ring. You have no imagination.
- Why not agree to a marriage based on love? A cruise to the Marquesas Islands, a honeymoon in Bora Bora?
- Me — agree to tie the knot? Not a chance! Marriage spells boredom; I deserve so much more!
- But what? I don't understand.
- A delicious meal, a beautifully set table, with candles and flowers. Folly, the quiver of sensual delight, frolicking, gambolling and romping about. Offer me delicacies, oysters and chocolate; champagne, caviar, fine wines, and nougat for dessert. Offer me excess. Offer to punish my body with the delights of this earth. I will open my arms and so much more to you. I will bring you to heights far, far beyond your wildest imaginings.

(to be continued)

... and a Few Good Dishes

Brochettes of Marinated Shrimp and Scallops

- 1¹/₂ cups/200 g large fresh shrimp
- 1¹/₂ cups/200 g large fresh scallops
- 1 cup/250 ml clam juice
- 2 tablespoons lime juice
- 6 dashes of Worcestershire sauce
- red, yellow and green peppers, cubed
1. In a glass dish approximately 1 inch (3 cm) deep, combine the clam juice, lime juice and Worcestershire sauce.
2. Marinate the shrimp and scallops in the mixture for 1 hour.
3. Drain and set aside the marinade.
4. Thread the seafood and peppers on to pre-soaked wooden skewers and brush with the marinade.
5. Broil or barbecue for 3 to 5 minutes.
6. Serve on a bed of rice or noodles flavoured with pesto.

FOR DESSERT: Don't fret, don't overwork yourself, save your strength for later. Drop by your neighbourhood bakery and ask for the very finest, the very richest, the most sinful of chocolate pastries.

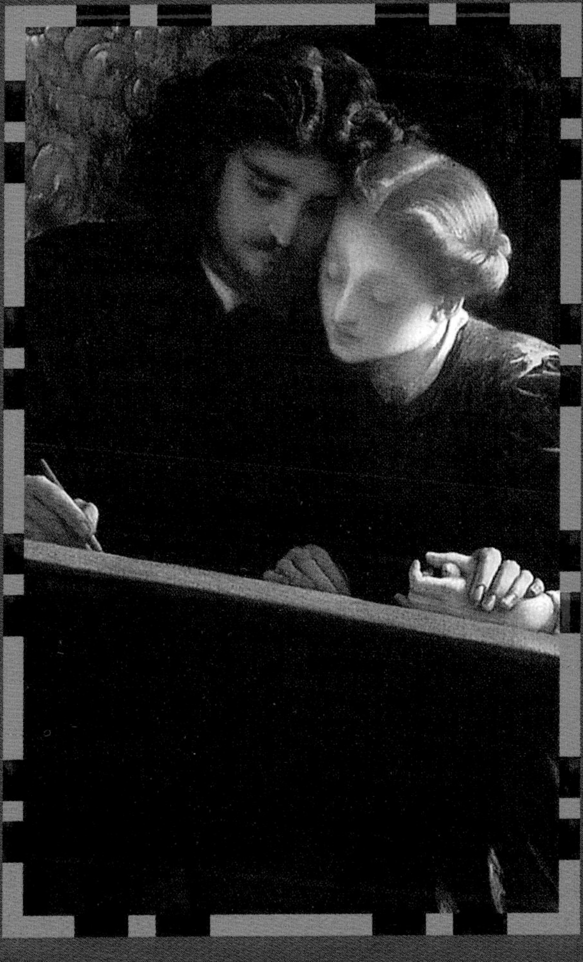

Male Fantasies

Your man has confessed that he fantasizes about the latest actress or the latest singer to hit the tabloids. Don't be insulted. The tendency is completely normal and carries no consequences. On the contrary! The women that men invent for themselves are always available, young, magnificently beautiful and expert in love's many games. But you have a tremendous advantage: you are real and you are part of his life. He responds to your advances, you are the woman he reaches out to touch, you are the woman he desires. Let him have his fantasies and share your own with him. The process will bring you closer.

Female Fantasies

A woman's imagination is very different from her male partner's, but many confirm that fantasies help them reach orgasm. The virtual lover who takes her on a moonlit beach or a forbidden and very public location is always the ideal lover! Men shouldn't take offence: the simple fact of imagining a partner with no drawbacks and no faults, against a dreamlike backdrop, encourages women to embrace abandon and to reach orgasm much more easily.

"We are all born for love. It is the principle of existence, and its only end."

Benjamin Disraeli

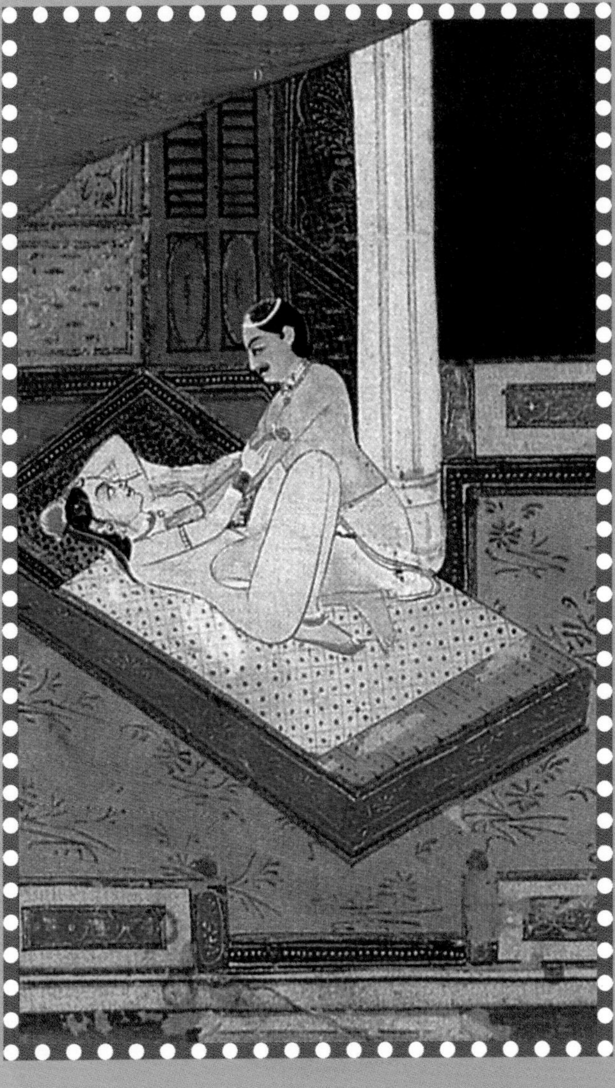

"Love looks not with the eyes, but with the mind;
And therefore is winged Cupid painted blind."

William Shakespeare

"All mankind loves a lover."

Ralph Waldo Emerson

"They do not love that do not show their love."

John Heywood

"Of all the pain, the greatest pain,
It is to love, but in vain."

Abraham Cowley

"They sin who tell us Love can die:
With Life all other passions fly,
All others are but vanity."

Robert Southey

"A man falls in love through his eyes
a woman through her ears."

Woodrow Wyatt

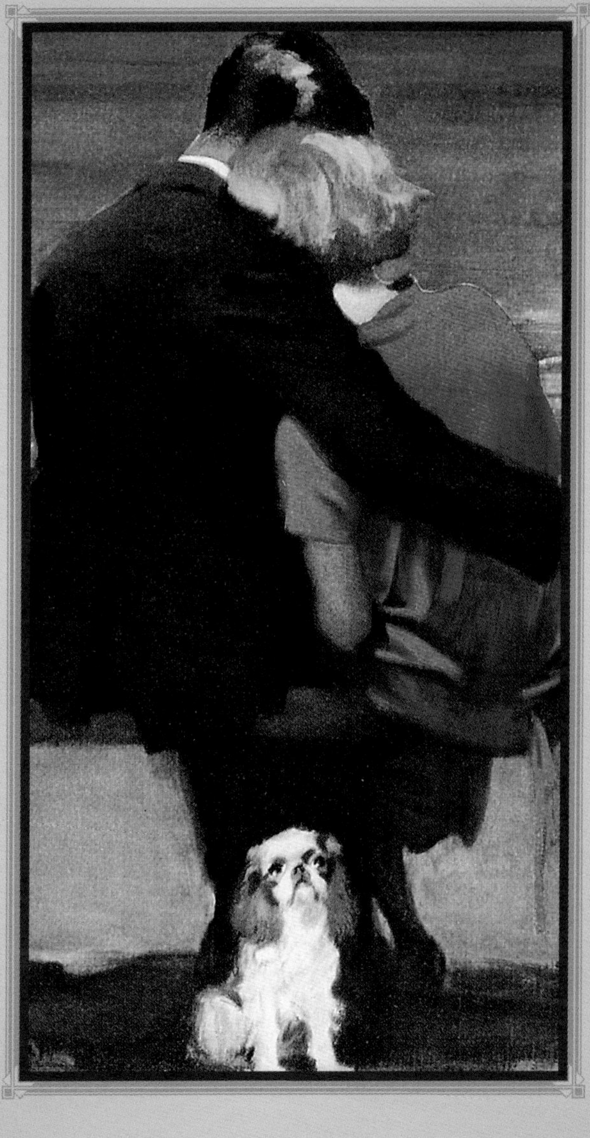

The Face of Desire

This morning, sitting alone on the sunny terrace, I felt the sudden rush of desire. It was an overwhelming feeling, the passage from icy cold to fiery warmth. Incapable of taking even the smallest step so captivated was I by the image of your body, I conjured your face, enveloped in the halo of your soul — my desire only increased. I felt the urgent need to see you, to look into your eyes, to take you in my arms to confirm that you do indeed exist, to confirm the reality that has changed my life forever, that has convinced me that eternity is a possibility and a certainty. At that very moment, I realized that the face, more than any other part of the body, is what sparks desire and what elicits the sublime and unalterable. At that very moment, I understood that you would forever be a part of my life.

L.T.

"For aught that I could ever read,
Could ever hear by tale or history,
The course of true love never did run smooth."

William Shakespeare

"And yet, to say the truth, reason and love
keep little company together now-a-days."

William Shakespeare

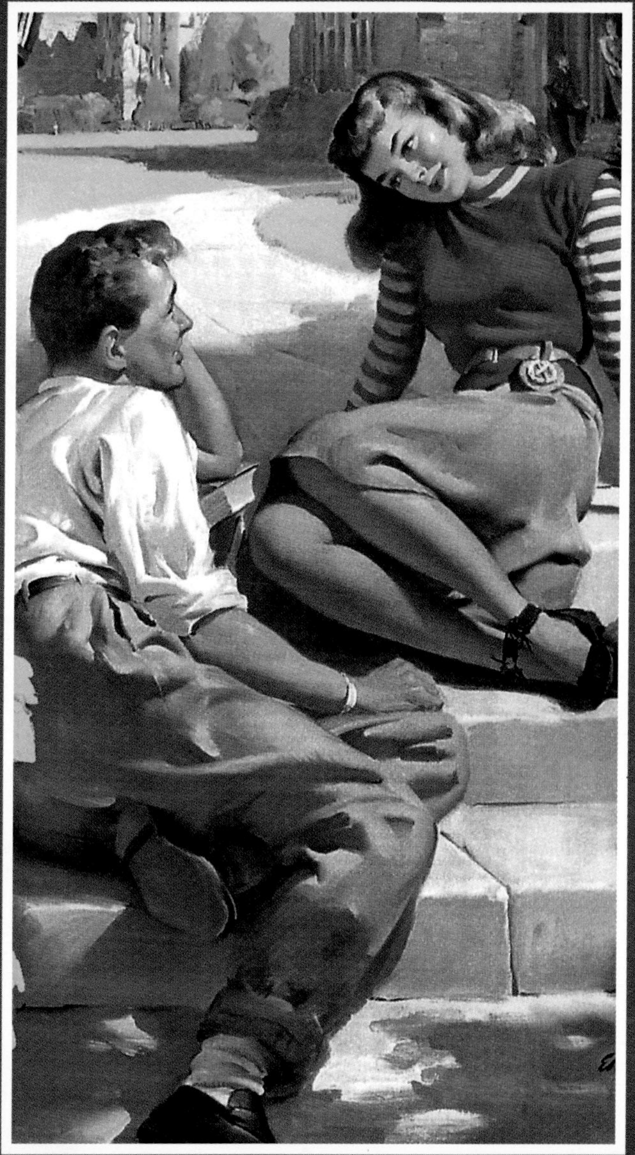

She Walks In Beauty

She walks in beauty, like the night
Of cloudless climes and starry skies;
And all that's best of dark and bright
Meet in her aspect and her eyes:
Thus mellow'd to that tender light
Which heaven to gaudy day denies.

One shade the more, one ray the less,
Had half impair'd the nameless grace
Which waves in every raven tress,
Or softly lightens o'er her face;
Where thoughts serenely sweet express
How pure, how dear their dwelling-place.

And on that cheek, and o'er that brow,
So soft, so calm, yet eloquent,
The smiles that win, the tints that glow,
But tell of days in goodness spent,
A mind at peace with all below,
A heart whose love is innocent!

Lord Byron

"The heart knows no wrinkles."

Madame de Sévigné

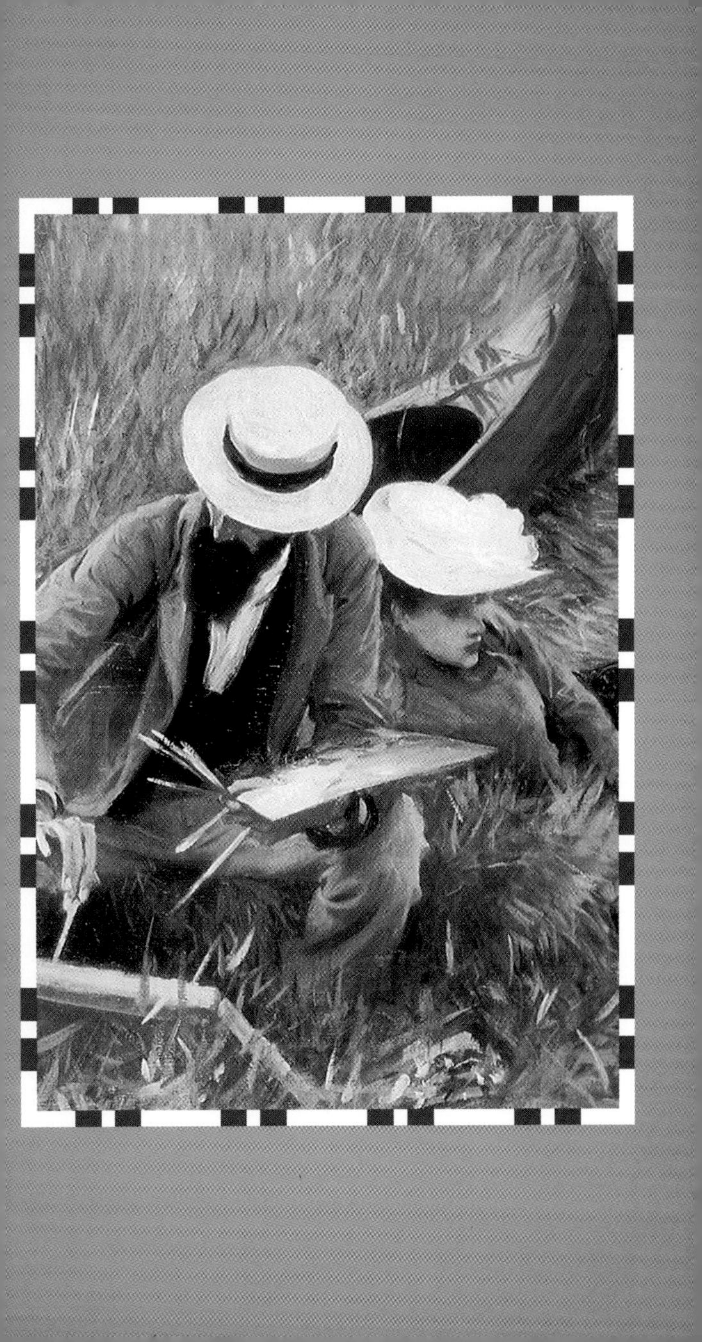

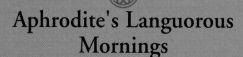

Aphrodite's Languorous Mornings

Champagne and Orange Juice

You've put your prettiest champagne flutes in the refrigerator the night before, the better to chill them before filling them with equal parts of fresh orange juice and iced champagne.

Oven-Baked Grapefruit

- 1 chilled pink grapefruit
- $^1/_4$ cup/50 g brown sugar
- 2 teaspoons unsalted butter
- 2 juicy, oversized strawberries

• Cut the grapefruit in half.
• Add 1 teaspoon of butter to the middle of each half.
• Sprinkle with brown sugar.
• In a buttered dish, bake at 350°F (180°C) for approximately 10 minutes.
• For maximum visual effect, serve on a lettuce leaf.

N.B.: Indulge as many fantasies as your imagination generates, and remember those that the body yearns for as well.

"Take! O take those lips away,
that so sweetly were forsworn;
And those eyes, the break of day,
Lights that do mislead the morn;
But my kisses bring again, bring again,
Seals of love, but seal'd in vain, seal'd in vain."

William Shakespeare

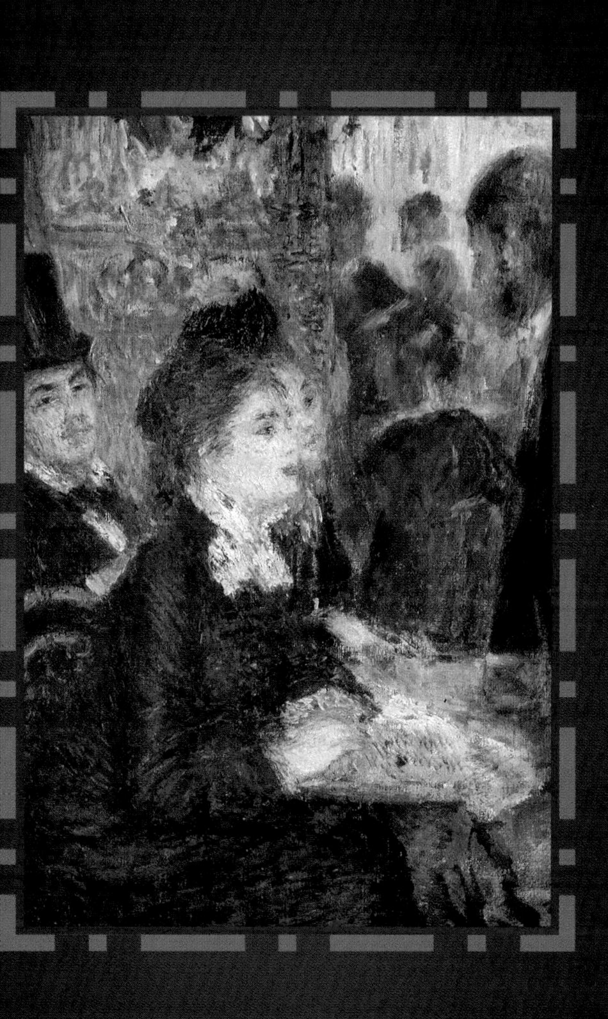

"Out of my thoughts! You are part of my
existence, part of myself. You have been in every
line I have ever read, since I first came here,
the rough common boy whose poor heart you
wounded even then. You have been in every
prospect I have ever seen since - on the river,
on the sails of the ships, on the marshes, in the
clouds, in the light, in the darkness, in the wind,
in the woods, in the sea, in the streets. You have
been the embodiment of every graceful fancy
that my mind has ever become acquainted with.
The stones of which the strongest London
buildings are made, are not more real, or more
impossible to be displaced by your hands, than
your presence and influence have been to me,
there and everywhere, and will be. Estella,
to the last hour of my life, you cannot choose
but remain part of my character, part of the
little good in me, part of the evil. But, in this
separation I associate you only with the good,
and I will faithfully hold you to that always,
for you must have done me far more good than
harm, let me feel now what sharp distress I may.
O God bless you, God forgive you!"

Charles Dickens

The Song of Songs

Behold, thou art fair, my love;
behold, thou art fair;
thou hast doves' eyes
within thy locks:
thy hair is as a flock of goats,
that appear from mount Gilead.

Thy teeth are like a flock of sheep
that are even shorn,
which came up from the washing;
whereof every one bear twins,
and none is barren among them.

Thy lips are like a thread of scarlet,
and thy speech is comely:
thy temples are like a piece of a
pomegranate within thy locks.

Thy neck is like the tower of David
builded for an armoury,
whereon there hang a thousand
bucklers, all shields of mighty men.

Thy two breasts
are like two young roes
that are twins,
which feed among the lilies.

The Bible (excerpt)

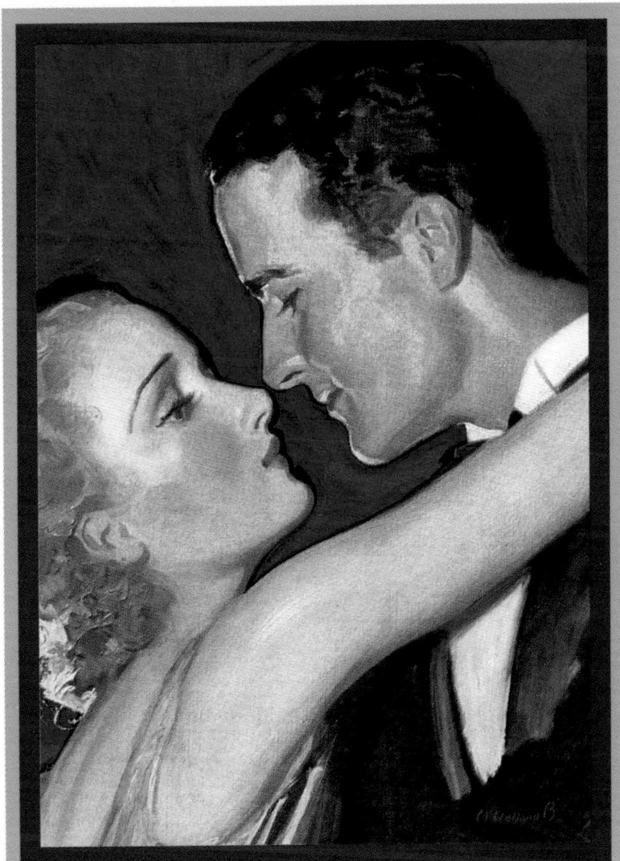

The Passionate Shepherd
to His Love

Come live with me and be my Love,
And we will all the pleasures prove
That hills and valleys, dales and fields,
Or woods or sleepy mountain yields.

And we will sit upon the rocks,
And see the shepherds feed their flocks
By shallow rivers, to whose falls
Melodious birds sing madrigals.

And I will make thee beds of roses
And a thousand fragrant posies;
A cap of flowers, and a kirtle
Embroidered all with leaves of myrtle;

A gown made of the finest wool
Which from our pretty lambs we pull;
Fair-lined slippers for the cold,
With buckles of the purest gold;

A belt of straw and ivy buds
With coral clasps and amber studs:
And if these pleasures may thee move
Come live with me and be my Love.

The shepherd swains shall dance and sing
For thy delight each May morning:
If these delights thy mind may move,
Then live with me and be my Love.

Christopher Marlowe

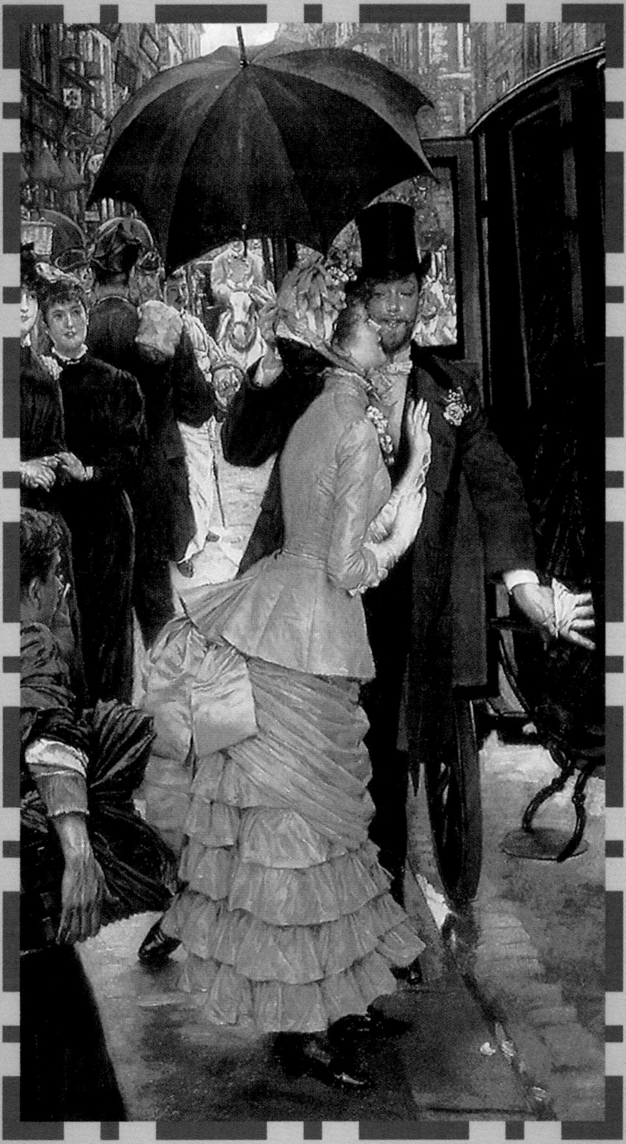

The Nymph's Reply to the Shepherd

If all the world and love were young,
And truth in every shepherd's tongue,
These pretty pleasures might me move
To live with thee and be thy love.

Time drives the flocks from field to fold
When rivers rage and rocks grow cold,
And Philomel becometh dumb;
The rest complains of cares to come.

The flowers do fade, and wanton fields
To wayward winter reckoning yields;
A honey tongue, a heart of gall,
Is fancy's spring, but sorrow's fall.

Thy gowns, the shoes, thy beds of roses,
Thy cap, the kirtle, and thy posies,
Soon break, soon wither, soon forgotten —
In folly ripe, in reason rotten.

Thy belt of straw and ivy buds,
Thy coral clasps and amber studs,
All these in me no means can move
To come to thee and be thy love.

But could youth last and love still breed,
Had joys no date nor age no need,
Then these delights my mind might move
To live with thee and be thy love.

Sir Walter Raleigh

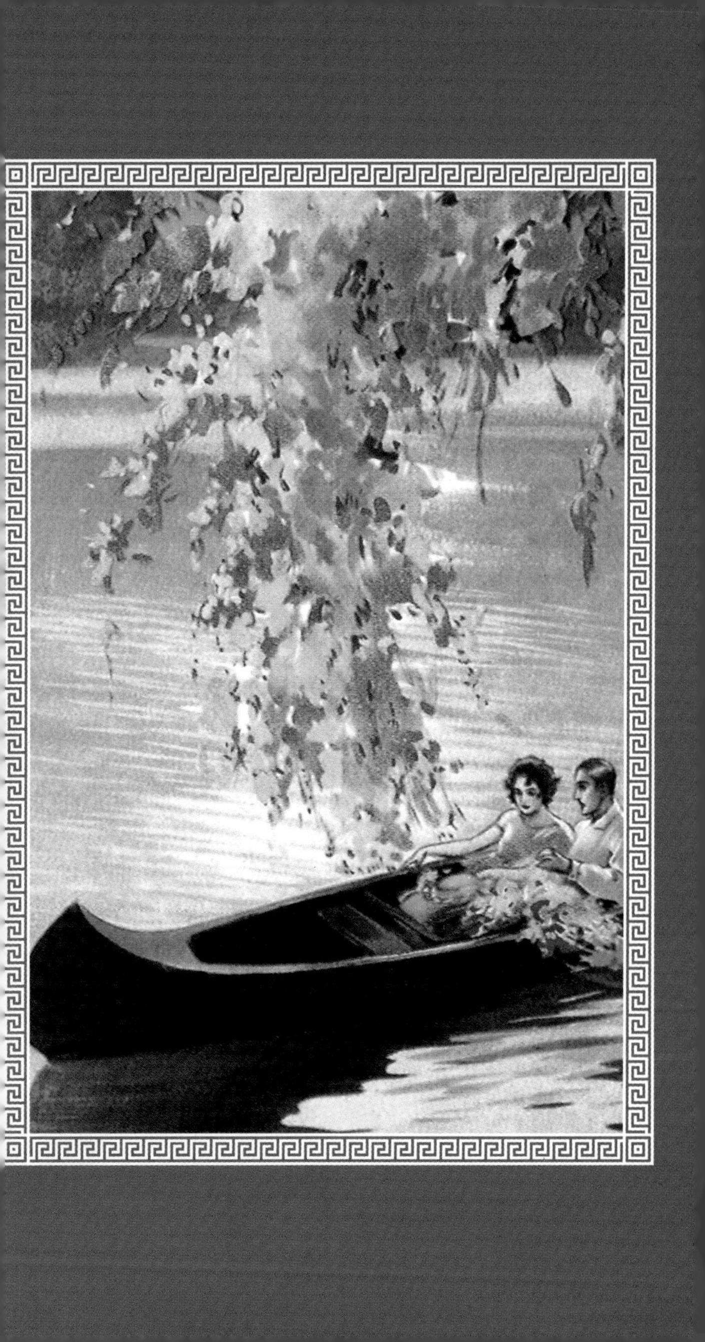

Love is a strange feeling that links us mysteriously to someone, tho
are unable to explain why or how. It is made of a thousand subtle
tions, a thousand almost imperceptible details that combined, create
sitivity that is heightened by the mere presence of the that other,
person who transforms and lifts our reality into another realm. Whe
feel confident that you can take on any challenge life may bring you
when you are sure that you can move mountains, your friends ine
think that you are officially in love. And strangely but similarly, whe
look tormented or melancholic, when you complain that life is dreary

gray,
concer
parad
we are
love k
sought
with th
delirio
with th
uncert
being.
we ma
ng th
why or
imperc
by the

lifts our reality into another realm. When you feel confident that yo
ake on any challenge life may bring your way, when you are sure th
can move mountains, your friends inevitably think that you are off
in love. And strangely but similarly, when you look tormented or m
cholic, when you complain that life is dreary and gray, those same f
will suspect that love is the cause of all your concerns. Love, tho
exalting, more often than not plunges us into a paradoxical state whe
and sadness alternate. However, even when we are in an extreme st
doubt as to the sincerity of our "other one", love keeps us loyal, love